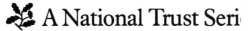 A National Trust Seri

Knights and _ ___

THE INSIDE STORY OF
KING ARTHUR AND THE ROUND TABLE

Harry T Sutton

BATSFORD – HERITAGE BOOKS

Research: R J Sutton

Design and art direction: Fetherstonhaugh Associates, London

Illustrations: Chapters 1 and 2, Chris Molan; Chapters 3,
Valerie Headland and Judith Jeffery

Copyright © 1978 by B T Batsford Limited and Heritage Books

Produced by Heritage Books

Published jointly by B T Batsford Limited and Heritage Books

Distributed by B T Batsford Limited, 4 Fitzhardinge Street,
London W1H 0AH

Printed by Robert MacLehose & Co. Ltd, Glasgow

ISBN 0 7134 1731 5

Contents

1 Gareth and the Red Knight

It was a long ride on horseback to Camelot. Shortlegs was tired and could no longer hide his impatience.

'If you want to become a knight you'll have to be a good deal brighter than that,' he said scornfully. 'King Arthur would never fall for such a simple trick.'

'It's the best one I can think of,' said Gareth. 'What do you suggest instead?'

The dwarf looked pityingly up at his tall friend. 'King Arthur is your uncle – right?' he asked.

'Yes,' agreed Gareth.

'And Sir Gawain, one of his best knights, is your brother – true?'

'Yes, he is.'

'Well then – it's perfectly simple. We arrive at Camelot as complete strangers seeking help. You persuade King Arthur to let you live at court – say for a year. When an opportunity comes you prove yourself as brave as your brother and the king will be bound to make you a knight. Then you can tell him who you are and he will be delighted to find that it was his own nephew whom he chose for a knighthood. And we shall live happily ever after!'

The dwarf smiled cheerfully at his own cleverness and Gareth, too, was impressed. But then he had some doubts.

'Suppose I am recognised when we first arrive,' he objected. 'They will simply say that I am too young to be a knight and send me home.'

Shortlegs almost fell off his little horse with impatience.

'Your brother left home when you were only five years old,' he reminded Gareth, 'and your uncle Arthur has not set eyes on you since you were born. How could they possibly recognise you now?'

'Well,' said Gareth. 'Maybe I'll do as you say.'

But really there was no doubt in his mind at all. He would

do exactly as the dwarf said – as he always had since they were children together in the castle which had been their home.

Gareth's father, a rich nobleman, had given Shortlegs to him as a companion. Now they were both fifteen years old, but whereas Gareth was more than six feet tall and strong as a young ox, Shortlegs had not grown at all. Yet although he was only a dwarf, Gareth knew that his friend was far cleverer than himself and now, as they approached King Arthur's court, he also knew that he would take the dwarf's advice.

At King Arthur's castle of Camelot, the Knights of the Round Table were hungry and their tempers were becoming short.

'Every Whitsuntide it's the same thing,' complained Sir Launcelot. 'The food is cooked, the Round Table is laid and the wine jugs filled to the brim. Then the King makes us wait until we are almost starved to death.'

'Yes,' agreed Sir Gawain. 'But you must agree that when the feast does start at last, the King *is* proved right.'

It was indeed true that the feast always did take place in the end but the knights knew they would have a long wait when each year the King said the same thing: 'I shall not break bread until some marvel or news of a great adventure is shown me!'

And everybody about the court had to think hard about marvels and adventures. But it was always difficult to find one that would please the King. On this particular Whitsunday, the very day that Gareth and Shortlegs were on their way to Camelot, news of marvels and adventures was especially hard to find and the knights were hungrier than they had ever been before.

'Oh, please God, let an adventure come our way,' prayed the knights and the sweet smell of cooking – roasted ox, venison, and wild boar – drifted up from the kitchens to make their hunger worse. Even the King himself was becoming impatient and wondering whether, this time, the feast might not take place at all, when there were cheerful shouts and Sir Gawain and Sir Launcelot came into the hall.

'There is a great marvel at our very castle gates, my lord,' they told the King. 'A youth has come, a tall, fair youth, attended only by a dwarf. The two demand entrance to the castle for they say the youth has business with the King!'

'A youth and a dwarf you say,' said the King. And he laughed with delight at the idea. 'Are they armed, this fearsome pair? Do they come as friends we should welcome or as enemies we must fear?'

There was laughter too amongst the knights at this, for none could imagine famous King Arthur afraid of anything or anyone – especially not a dwarf and a youth however fierce might be their demands.

'We shall not know, my lord, until we hear the nature of their business with Your Grace,' said Sir Launcelot. Then he glanced round at the rows of hungry knights and the food piled high on the table behind. 'But be assured, sire,' he said, 'they will prove marvellous enough to give you pleasure at the feast!'

'You are hungry too, Sir Launcelot,' laughed the King.

Then he beckoned Sir Kay, his steward.

'Bring them to me,' he said. 'And let the feast begin.'

Halting their horses at the moat of King Arthur's castle at Camelot, Gareth and Shortlegs rehearsed the parts they were to play.

'Remember to look hungry,' whispered the dwarf. 'Lean on me for support as though you can barely stand!'

'What shall I do if the King says no?' Gareth whispered back. But their discussion was interrupted by a man's voice from the far side of the moat. It was one of the guards.

'Who are you and what do you want at King Arthur's castle?' shouted the man.

'We have business with the King and only with him shall we speak,' Shortlegs shouted back. They heard the man laugh and he turned away as though he could not be bothered further with such an unlikely pair; but then he was joined by two other men. The castle moat was wide but even from where they stood, Gareth and Shortlegs could see that the newcomers were two of Arthur's knights for they were dressed in courtly clothes as if for a feast. The two knights looked across the water at them for a moment; then they went off. Minutes later the great drawbridge began to move down, its massive timbers groaning under the strain of heavy chains. And as Gareth and the dwarf rode across, the portcullis was lifted to give them entrance to Camelot, the most famous castle in the world.

'Remember – you are weak with hunger,' whispered Shortlegs.

'And I want a place at court,' added Gareth. Then a servant took their horses and moments later they were in King Arthur's hall.

Before them as they entered was the great Round Table and seated at it the knights of Arthur's court. Here, gathered in one place, were more than a hundred of the bravest knights in the world. Now that the feast was to begin the ladies of the court were also at the table; their beauty and the finery of their

clothes adding elegance to the brilliant scene. There amongst them, set apart only by the gold circlet he wore in place of a crown, was King Arthur, the most valiant knight of all. And next to him, Queen Guinevere, the most beautiful of all the ladies. It was to them that Gareth now made his way and Shortlegs, knowing that his small part was played, stayed behind, watching and hoping that his young friend would not fail.

Silence fell as the knights stared with interest at the handsome youth who dared to make this lone approach to the King. Although he was so young, Gareth looked strong as any man. His shoulders were broad in proportion to his height, his hair was fair as ripened corn, his arms muscular, his wrists powerful and his bearing, as he walked towards the King, was of one born to the freedom of the open air. Yet for all his strength, his hands were slender as a girl's; a certain sign that this youth had never laboured on the land.

'Here, surely,' the knights told themselves, 'must be a nobleman's son.'

Going directly to the King and Queen, Gareth knelt before them and bowed his head in respect.

'Great King,' he said, and the words came strangely to his

own ears as he came face to face with his famous uncle at last. 'I have three gifts to ask of you. One I ask for now and the other two in one year's time.' Then he hesitated and looking anxiously at the King, added: 'They will be gifts, sire, which you will be easily able to grant.'

Queen Guinevere smiled and the King's eyes twinkled as he heard these last words. The knights around him laughed aloud for it was indeed hard to imagine three gifts so rare that they could not be granted by King Arthur.

'Ask on, young man,' said the King kindly, 'and you shall have all you ask.'

In his excitement, Gareth forgot the plans he had made with Shortlegs. He forgot to look half-starved; he forgot that he should appear too weak to stand. He looked, as he really was, an extremely healthy young man, strong and quite able to hold his own even before the Knights of the Round Table. His next words to the King were, therefore, a great surprise for he said, simply:

'My first request, my lord, is for food and drink at your court for one year and at that year's end I shall ask for the other gifts.'

There was more laughter at the table at this and King Arthur himself looked amused for it was well known that there was always food and drink at Camelot for all who came, friend and enemy alike. This was the normal custom of England's Christian king.

'This is no gift, my son, but your right as a visitor to my court,' said the King. 'Ask on, for I can see that you are of gentle birth and it will please me to grant you a gift more worthy of your father's undoubted noble name.'

'That is all I ask, my lord,' said Gareth.

The King looked puzzled. So did Queen Guinevere.

'What is your name, young man?' she asked.

'That, madam, I cannot say,' said Gareth, and he looked anxiously at her to see if she had guessed the truth.

But she and the King only smiled, for such a mystery was very much to both their tastes. Calling his steward, Sir Kay, to him the King said: 'I put this nameless youth in your charge.

See that he has food and drink of the best kind and a place to sleep worthy of one of noble birth, for such I believe he will prove.'

Sir Kay, however, was more cautious.

'Your Grace may be deceived,' he told the King. 'The youth may seem of gentle birth yet he asks not for armour and horse, as would befit one born to knighthood, but for food and drink – the needs of a mere peasant. He is a rogue who will rob you and run away, my lord. Send him packing from the court!'

At these words, Sir Launcelot sprang to his feet. He pointed a warning hand to Sir Kay: 'You will regret those words,' he told him. 'The boy may not have a name but he has the bearing of a brave man. Do as the King commands I say!'

Sir Kay, his face flushed with anger, now turned to Gareth and his voice was scornful as he said:

'So, you have no name you say? Then I shall name you Beaumains – Prettyhands, for your hands are those of a woman not a man. And you shall have food in plenty – in the kitchens

where you will work with the lads and serving wenches for your year at Arthur's court!'

And although Gareth flushed angrily at his words, he merely bowed to Sir Kay as would any apprentice boy given orders which he had to obey. Then the Knights of the Round Table and their ladies went back to their feast and the King turned to talk of adventures far more exciting than the arrival of such a handsome but weak-kneed youth. Gareth went to the doorway of the hall to join the scullions who were to be his companions for a year.

'How now, Prettyhands,' said one of them as he approached. 'Here is your first food at Arthur's court,' and he threw Gareth a meat bone which had already been gnawed by one of the well-fed hunting dogs.

Sadly, but without complaint, Gareth took the bone.

'Thank you for your kindness, sir,' he said to the lad. And he tossed the bone back to the dog.

It had been a long year for Shortlegs. Separated from his life-long friend, he had spent the time at Gareth's home, awaiting the day when he might return to Camelot and complete the plan. From time to time he had news of Gareth and always it was of his friend's sufferings at the hands of Sir Kay; but always also he heard of Gareth's patience and goodwill in the face of insult and ill treatment and knew that he was proving himself worthy of the first demands of knighthood – courage in adversity and loyalty to one's lord and master.

But other things he had heard as well. Of Gareth's successes at contests held at court – tests of strength, of throwing and wrestling – which he always won. And of how he was once chosen by Sir Gawain to be his squire at a jousting contest at the court.

Now, as Whitsuntide approached once more, the dwarf was on his way to Camelot riding the small pony which was all his short shanks could manage and leading a fine charger, the gift of Gareth's mother to her son. Strapped to the charger's saddle was a suit of armour – and a sword – the shining steel

glinting in the sun.

Along the road, Shortlegs met some other travellers to Camelot. A lady with men-at-arms attending her, she looked curiously at the dwarf as he rode up beside her.

'Good day, my lady,' said Shortlegs. 'Do you, like me, travel to King Arthur's court? If you do, we can go in company together.'

The lady smiled at the dwarf's impertinence for the very idea of travelling with such a tiny person as companion was really too absurd! But the little fellow seemed harmless enough and, as she was in need of conversation, she replied:

'Gladly, sir, will I accept your company for indeed I do go to Camelot to seek King Arthur's help.'

'Tell me what help you want from the King, for I have a friend at the court,' Shortlegs told her, importantly. 'It may be that if I ask him, he would further your cause.'

The Lady Lyonet, for that was her name, laughed at the dwarf's words; amused that so small a figure could have such big ideas.

'To be sure,' she said. 'I hope to find a Knight of the Round Table to kill a cruel tyrant who has already defeated more knights than I can count on the fingers of both hands. Perhaps you can find for me such a knight?'

'Certainly,' said Shortlegs. 'I know of such a knight – or one soon to be a knight who, if I ask him, will gladly despatch your tyrant for you. I shall tell him of your need when we reach Camelot.'

The Whitsuntide feast, this year, was not delayed. Soon after dawn a messenger had arrived at Arthur's court to herald the arrival of the Lady Lyonet, and being made welcome on her arrival, she was soon shown to the great hall where she made her appeal to King Arthur and all the Round Table Knights.

'What lady is threatened by this tyrant?' asked the King when he had heard the Lady Lyonet's request. 'What is her name and where is the castle where she is kept a prisoner?'

'The lady is my sister, sire,' she told him, 'and the tyrant is called the Red Knight . . .'

Before she could say more, a wave of excited talk swept the room, for the name 'Red Knight' was familiar to all who sat at the Round Table as the most cruel and dangerous villain that lived. At once there was a chorus of demands from the knights –

'Send me, my lord, to rescue this lady from the Red Knight . . .'

'No, I claim the adventure, my lord . . .'

But then, in the midst of the clamour, there was a commotion at the entrance to the hall and in strode Gareth. He went straight to where King Arthur stood with the Lady Lyonet and, as silence fell on the hall, declared in a loud clear voice:

'This adventure, my lord, I claim as your promised second gift!'

There were cries of – 'the kitchen boy pretends to be a knight!' and 'Prettyhands would be eaten by the Red Knight!' But King Arthur silenced them.

'I have promised this youth a second gift and this I must grant.'

Then turning to Lady Lyonet he said: 'Here is your champion, fair damsel. He is yours to command.'

But the Lady Lyonet flushed angrily at his words. 'I came to Camelot to seek the aid of a famous knight, not the plate scourings from your kitchen, sire,' she said. 'Send this scullion back to his spit-turning and I will seek elsewhere for the help my sister needs.' And she stormed off, leaving Gareth flushed and shamefaced at her scornful words. Then, as though to add a final blow to Gareth's shame, across the hall came Shortlegs, Gareth's helmet on his head and the rest of the armour and the sword held under both short arms. He looked a comic figure and a roar went round the hall as the Knights of the Round Table laughed until tears filled their eyes. In the midst of the uproar, Sir Launcelot sprang up from his place and shouted:

'Shame on you for laughing at this brave youth,' and he turned to the King. 'I will go with him to be his squire on this adventure, my lord, for I swear that he will prove to be a

champion worthy of a place at our table.' Then he looked angrily at his companions. 'He will show himself to be no kitchen boy but a true knight who will return one day to avenge himself upon you laughing fools!'

Gareth turned to him in gratitude and said:

'Thank you, sir, for your offer of help, but I must meet this adventure alone.' Then, turning to the King, he said: 'Sire, the third gift that I ask for is a knighthood at Sir Launcelot's hands when I have proved my worth!'

'That gift, also, shall be yours,' said the King.

The Lady Lyonet was furious. It was bad enough that King Arthur should insult her with the offer of a kitchen boy to be her knight. But even worse, she had hardly started her journey away from Camelot when the kitchen boy and his dwarf caught up with her. The fact that the youth was now dressed in

armour and mounted on a fine steed did not lessen the insult.

'What do you want, scullion?' she asked, as he rode up to her side. 'You stink of greasy pans and cooking pots. I want no help from you!'

'Madam,' said Gareth, 'the King has granted me your adventure and that I shall undertake; at the cost of my life if need be. You shall not turn me away.'

'And, madam,' added Shortlegs, 'I shall go with my master to see that he is ready for battle when the time comes!'

But the Lady Lyonet would not be persuaded.

'I shall have nothing to do with you,' she said. And she rode away. Not knowing quite how to deal with the situation, Gareth and the dwarf dropped back on their horses and followed a distance away.

'What now?' asked Gareth, gloomily.

'Something will turn up,' replied Shortlegs. 'It always does.'

Sir Launcelot, mounted and armed, set off from the castle along the way that Gareth and the dwarf had gone.

'Please God I shall not be too late,' he muttered to himself, and he spurred his horse into a gallop to make up the wasted time.

When the feast ended, talk had turned to Gareth and the Lady Lyonet. One of the knights remembered that the youth had been armed only with a sword and that had led to a remark by Sir Kay.

'My kitchen boy could not use a lance if he had one – it would spoil his pretty hands!' he had said. And then he added: 'Nor will he need a shield for he will not go near enough to a fight to meet a blow!'

'You are wrong,' Sir Launcelot had told him; and flaring into a temper, Sir Kay had replied:

'So be it then. I will take the kitchen boy my own lance and shield and if he can win it from me he will be properly armed for battle!' Then, quickly putting on his armour, he had gone off in pursuit of Gareth, clearly looking for a fight.

Now, pressing his horse to its fastest speed, Sir Launcelot was also in hot pursuit. 'I fear that I may be too late,' he told himself. And his sweating horse once more felt the urging prick of spurs.

The first Gareth knew of Sir Kay's approach was a clatter of hooves on the hard road behind and a taunting voice which called:

'Do you not recognise me, Sir Prettyhands? Are you too proud in your borrowed armour to greet an old friend?'

Recognising the voice, Gareth replied at once.

'I know you well, Sir Kay, as one who has been my enemy this whole year past. And now look you to your defence for I shall have my revenge!'

Then turning his horse, Gareth drew his sword and charged full tilt, not stopping even to close the visor of his helmet so eager was he for the fight. Sir Kay, taken by surprise, had not time even to level his lance at the charging figure who now bore

down on him at a furious speed. Gareth's sword found a gap beneath his enemy's breastplate and when he withdrew it, there was blood on the blade. Sir Kay fell from his horse and lay still.

Quickly dismounting, Shortlegs ran to the fallen knight and snatched up his lance and shield; he handed them to Gareth.

'First spoils of battle, master,' he said, and in the dwarf's voice there was a new note of respect.

Sir Launcelot was just in time to see Sir Kay's defeat and he was about to shout a word of praise to the kitchen boy turned swordsman when he in turn, found himself attacked. Turning to see another knight approaching, Gareth mistook him for an enemy. Levelling his newly won lance, he again charged full tilt.

So fierce was the exchange of lance thrusts that both riders were unseated and fell to the ground.

'Defend yourself!' shouted Gareth, getting to his feet and drawing his sword. Sir Launcelot had to fight hard to defend himself from the furious youth and once he was nearly disarmed by a savage swing of Gareth's sword. At last Sir

Launcelot called a halt.

'We have no quarrel, you and I,' he said, lifting his visor so that Gareth could see his face.

'Forgive me!' cried Gareth, amazed to discover who he had been fighting.

'You are forgiven, fair youth, and willingly,' replied Sir Launcelot. Then he added:

'You have earned your last gift from King Arthur, but before I make you a knight, you must tell me your true name.'

'I am Gareth, brother to Sir Gawain and nephew to the King.'

'And I am Shortlegs, his friend,' said the dwarf.

'Then I dub you Sir Gareth,' said Sir Launcelot, placing his sword blade on the proud youth's shoulder. 'And you, sir dwarf, I name this knight's true squire!'

'And I,' declared the Lady Lyonet, who had watched both combats with amazement and pride, 'I declare you my champion against the Red Knight!'

Dame Lyoness sat in the window of her chamber in the castle tower and shed bitter tears. For many long weeks her sister, the Lady Lyonet, had been gone and every day since, Dame Lyoness had looked to see her return. Beyond the moat she could see the tents of the Red Knight and his men who had laid siege to her castle, hoping that she, with her servants and men-at-arms, would at last surrender. And daily she looked in the direction from which she hoped one of King Arthur's knights would come riding to aid her.

She was almost in despair when at last a servant came to her and said: 'Mistress, there is a dust cloud on the road towards Camelot and every minute it comes closer. Please God – help may be coming at last!' And drying her tears, Dame Lyoness ran to the window from where she could clearly see the distant road and, sure enough, she could make out the figure of a knight in armour; and a few yards behind she saw her sister. It was true. Help had come.

But even as she watched, trumpets sounded in the Red Knight's camp, and Dame Lyoness saw the tyrant himself riding to meet the approaching knight.

'Come one pace closer, Sir Knight,' she heard him shout, 'and you will join that row of dead knights yonder!' And he pointed to the horrible sight of ten corpses, hanging from the nearby trees.

'They came too close,' he told Gareth – for, of course, the newcomer was he – 'and they tasted the Red Knight's sword. Go back from whence you came, or you shall taste it likewise!'

From her place, high up in the castle tower, Dame Lyoness could see all that now occurred.

Disdaining even a glance at the line of swinging corpses, the newcomer levelled his lance and charged fearlessly at the Red Knight. But the tyrant was ready. He held his seat against Gareth's furious onslaught. The clash of armour as both weapons found their marks told of the strength that each man brought to the fight – and which would end with the death of one.

Turning, they charged again. And again.

To the ladies watching breathlessly from the tower, it seemed

23

as if the struggle for victory would never end, but it was in truth only minutes later when, with one fearsome thrust, Gareth toppled the Red Knight from his horse.

Leaping from his saddle, sword in hand, he stood over the tyrant and cried: 'So, Sir Knight, do you meet the same fate as your many unhappy victims!' And with a mighty thrust his sword pierced the Red Knight's armour and found the tyrant's heart.

For a moment, Gareth stared at his dead enemy, then raising his visor, he saluted the lady in the castle tower, and called to her: 'Your tyrant is dead, fair damsel. I come now to kiss your hand.' And as the soldiers of the Red Knight fell back to let him pass, Sir Gareth rode across the drawbridge and entered the castle that had been so long besieged.

Shortlegs was Gareth's squire at his wedding when he married Dame Lyoness. His master bought him a brand new suit and a small sword to wear at his side, just for the occasion. And of course, the dwarf was proved right. They did, all three, live happily ever after.

2 The Inside Story

The story of Gareth and the Red Knight is only one of many about King Arthur and his Knights of the Round Table. There is another well-known story about a sword, wedged so tightly into a block of stone that nobody could pull it out. It was said that, one day, someone would come and pull it from the stone. That person would be king. Young Arthur tried, easily removed the sword, and was crowned king.

In another story, King Arthur killed a giant on St Michael's Mount and rescued a damsel the giant had held captive. There are also stories about Merlin who was a magician, and about Launcelot, Gawain, Percival and other Round Table knights.

They are all, of course, fairy tales which nobody believes. Yet the strange thing is that Arthur was a real person. He was not a king, nor did he have a round table. But he did exist and the best way to find out who he really was, is by telling another tale. This one is about war between the Britons and the Anglo-Saxons (English).

THE BATTLE OF BADON

'Faster – faster!' Gwyn, the Briton, urged his tired horse, 'we must reach Arthur before it is too late!'

He had been riding most of the day along the old Roman road and dusk was falling when he at last reached Arthur's fortress on Cadbury Hill. Gwyn looked curiously at the tall watch-towers and ramparts. A long time ago, he knew, there had been a village on top of the hill. The Romans, it was said, had levelled the buildings and destroyed the defences. The villagers were moved out and the place had been left deserted. Now as Gwyn rode up to the entrance gates, he could see that the hilltop was once more a strongly fortified place.

'Halt!' he heard a voice from the watch-tower. 'Dismount and approach to be recognised.'

Gwyn did as he was ordered.

'I bring a message for Arthur from his kinsman in the town of Bath,' he told the man. 'It is a matter of life or death!'

He waited while the great wooden doors were unbarred and then, as they swung open to admit him, he followed the direction pointed out by the watchman and found himself at the entrance to Arthur's hall.

It was a big, barn-like place and at first Gwyn could not see clearly through the smoke from the central hearth and the flaming torches all round the walls. Then, as he drew close, he saw Arthur – the Briton's famous war leader – seated at the head of a long table, its top littered with the remains of a great feast. Around Arthur were his picked warriors, the leaders of a thousand horsemen who had already fought and won many battles. They were singing, these brawny fighting men, keeping time with their wine jugs, swaying cheerfully on their hard benches in the way of men who are more than a little drunk.

Gwyn had to shout in order to make himself heard above the din.

'My lord!' he yelled. 'My lord, I have a message from your cousin . . .'

Arthur, who had been singing with the others, put down his

wine jug for a moment.

'We are celebrating, as you can see. But what is your message, my friend. Good news I hope?'

'Desperate news, my lord,' said Gwyn. The singing had stopped now and the men round the table were listening with Arthur.

'The English, sir,' said Gwyn. 'They are on the march again. Their army is encamped above Bath in the old fort on Little Solsbury Hill. Your cousin bids you march to his aid for he has but one hundred men and the English are in great strength.'

For a moment there was silence. Then Arthur rose to his feet and flinging his wine jug from him, he shouted: 'To arms, my lads! We ride for Bath!'

All that night at Cadbury there was frantic activity as a thousand horsemen prepared for battle. It was more than thirty miles from Cadbury to Bath, three hours' hard riding, and to reach there by dawn when the English could be most easily surprised meant a start not long after midnight. It was at an early hour, therefore, that the gates of Cadbury swung wide and, in the light of a full moon, Arthur's cavalry rode out with their famous leader at their head.

Down below in the village, sleeping children were awakened by the thunder of hooves and the clatter of armour as the horsemen went by.

''Tis only Arthur and his men, off again to fight the wicked English,' their parents told them. And they turned over to go to sleep again.

The ride through the night was an easy one for after a short cross-country stretch they reached the Fosse Way, a straight Roman road which ran direct as an arrow to Bath. The city, when they reached it just before dawn, was quiet and deserted, the old Roman houses crumbling with decay. At the city gate the guard told them the English were still on Little Solsbury Hill and had spent the previous day building a strong fence round the top. Hearing this, Arthur stopped only for his men to water their horses, then rode on, following the Fosse Way where it ran beside the river Avon to the base of Solsbury Hill.

The English position, when they reached it, proved to be even more strongly defended than they had feared. The hilltop had once been a fortress almost as strong as Cadbury; and there were still stone walls round the ramparts which the English had made stronger with a wooden fence and heavy gates. As dawn broke spears could be seen moving behind the fence as the defenders looked out for enemies in the growing light. They soon saw Arthur and his cavalry. Arrows began to fly from the hilltop and men's shouts reached the watching horsemen. Quietly, Arthur ordered his men back, beyond arrow range.

'Those slopes are too steep for horses,' he told them, 'we must lay siege and starve them out!'

Inside their fortress, the English watched and waited for three days. They were long and anxious days for there was little water on Solsbury Hill and, soon, there would be no food.

Arthur had set up camp near the hill and his force was now twice as strong for he had been joined by fighting men from other tribes whose kings had sent them to fight under his command. Never had the English dared to move so far from their base in Kent; and the Britons knew that at all costs they must be stopped.

Only by breaking out through those waiting lines of cavalry could they escape and, on the third day, the English made the attempt. Horns sounded within the fortress – the signal for an attack. Then the gates were flung open and they streamed down the hillside, their descent covered by a cloud of arrows from the fortress above.

The English were foot-soldiers who used horses only as beasts of burden, and they were easy targets for Arthur's mounted men. He waited until the English were on the flat ground below the hill, then he gave the order.

'Charge!'

And with the fierce shouts of men about to kill – or be killed, the Britons galloped into their enemy.

Arthur's men fought in the Roman way for Roman fighting

methods had been handed down, father to son, from the times when Britons had fought with the legions.

Unable to break through the charging horsemen who were so well drilled that they seemed to fight as one man, the English wavered and broke. If they ran, they were chased and struck down. If they stood and fought, they were killed. Nine hundred and sixty Englishmen died on the battlefield and who knows how many more were killed in the chase that followed.

It was a great victory for the Britons, and Arthur was the hero of them all.

HOW WE KNOW

That story is based upon the detective work of many scholars who have searched into old books and documents, and dug into the ground at ancient sites to unravel the mystery of Arthur. For he is one of the greatest mystery men of all time.

Nobody knows where he was born nor where he was buried when he died. Nothing that belonged to him has ever been found. Nobody who knew him when he was alive wrote down the facts about him, or if they did, their writings have been lost.

About a hundred years after Arthur's death, a monk, making a calendar of Easter Days, mentioned that the Battle of Badon took place in 499 AD, and he noted that Arthur and the Britons were the victors. Another entry in the monk's calendar was for the death of Arthur, which he put at 539 AD. These are the only two written clues to Arthur that have survived.

A few more clues, however, can be added to this slight information, for a lot is known about other events which took place around the year 499.

To understand what it was like at the time of the Battle of Badon, we have to go back and look at Britain in Roman times. The fact was, of course, that Britain had been part of the great Roman Empire where peace was kept by Roman soldiers stationed in well-built camps and forts. The country was criss-crossed with properly made roads joining towns and villages; there were rich farmers growing corn, raising cattle and moving their crops to market in horse-drawn wagons. There were harbours and lighthouses round the coasts; swimming baths and theatres in the towns. Tribes of Britons, all with their own kings, lived peacefully enough under Roman rule; and many of them lived like Romans in farmhouses and mansions built in the Roman style.

It is not surprising, therefore, that some less fortunate peoples who lived outside Britain were envious of this prosperous land. The Anglo-Saxons especially – the English in the story – were determined to grab a share. They were a warlike race who lived in the harsher lands which are now southern Denmark and West Germany. Even while the Roman legions were in Britain, the English made armed raids along the east coasts making Roman rule very difficult. But when the Romans left to defend their own homeland in about 410 AD, the Britons had to look after themselves, and one British king made the mistake of asking the English for help in fighting tribes who were invading Britain from the north. In return, the English were to be allowed to settle in Kent and, once there, of course, these warlike people began to spread.

Used to the Roman way of life, the Britons detested the rough uncivilised English and fought hard to keep them back. But they could not be stopped and, year after year, they moved further west and north from Kent, killing and destroying and taking over land from Britons who simply had to give up and move away – or be killed.

This is the picture of life in Britain, revealed by old documents and excavations, until 499 – the Battle of Badon. Then, quite suddenly, it all changed. There were no more reports of English victories. Nothing was heard of the English in Britain for more than forty years. But there was news of them back on the Continent. Many had left Britain and were trying their luck elsewhere – in France. They had been defeated at the Battle of Badon and driven back in the fighting that almost certainly followed.

That, probably, is how Arthur became a national hero. He fought a battle which was a real 'Battle of Britain'; and turned the English back just in time. When they did return, more than forty years later, they were far less savage in their behaviour and, before long, settled down happily with the

Britons as their neighbours.

SEARCH FOR FACTS

People interested in the past are seldom satisfied with dry old documents and musty books. They like to find real evidence. Ancient swords left buried at the scene of a battle; cannon-balls, skeletons of people and, of course, buried treasure. Such things can only be found at places where historical events once happened. Cadbury Castle, in Somerset, has always been thought of as the site of King Arthur's castle of Camelot; and there is a village nearby called Queen Camel which makes it seem more likely. To find the truth, a party of archaeologists went there in 1966 and dug into the fortifications. They discovered some exciting things.

They found evidence that the hilltop had been re-fortified in about 480 AD after being deserted for several hundred years. They also uncovered the foundations of a feasting hall big enough for a great war leader and his warriors. They even found a very ancient wine bottle buried in the hall. Arthur might have had wine from it himself! Cadbury was not Camelot, nor a royal palace; but it could have been one of the camps Arthur used in his war against the English. Perhaps it was a strong base to which he could return to rest his men and prepare for the next battle. If this is true, Arthur would have

been copying the Roman legions who had just such garrisons at Caerleon, Chester and York.

The final mystery is where did the Battle of Badon really take place? There is nowhere in Britain that has that name today so we must look at the word Badon and see what it means. In one book, written in Latin not long after Arthur's death, it is called 'Mons Badonicus', which means Bath Hill. We also know that in the years before the Battle of Badon the English had moved into the upper reaches of the River Thames; and if you trace the Thames on a map you will find that its source is not far from Cirencester. The Fosse Way, built by the Romans, runs directly from Cirencester to Bath, and so it would have been easy for the English if they were near Cirencester, to head that way. If they did, and their intention was to grab some of the fertile land in the west, Little Solsbury Hill, just outside Bath, would have been a very good stopping place. Or, even more likely, a base for the battles they planned to fight against the Britons.

Other places have been suggested as the site of Badon. Badbury Rings in Dorset, and Badbury in Wiltshire are two. But the archaeologists working at Cadbury Castle in 1966 studied the problem and they concluded that the Battle of Badon was most likely to have been fought on a hill near Bath. And Little Solsbury could have been the hill.

THE FACTS
The truth about Arthur, then, is that he was a Briton who fought several battles against the English after the Romans left. The Battle of Badon, in which he defeated the English, was so important that he became a national hero in his lifetime.

But the odd thing is that he is not remembered for the Battle of Badon at all. He is famous for the Round Table – which never existed; for rescuing ladies in peril and killing giants and dragons – which he never did; and for being an *English* king – which was the last thing he could have been. As King Arthur he is, in fact, a legend; and the last part of the Inside Story is how that came about.

THE LEGEND

When an author wants to write a story, he first looks for a character; then for a plot. A good character for a story is one to whom exciting things can be made to happen. James Bond, for example, is an excellent character because, as '007' he had 'a licence to kill'. This meant that his author could make him murder anybody he liked, without Bond being sent to prison for life! Dr Who is another character around whom all kinds of adventures can be written.

King Arthur, with knights to be sent off on dangerous missions, and damsels in captivity waiting to be rescued, is even better. If the author gets his hero into such trouble that he cannot find a way out, he can just call up Merlin and a little magic will sort the whole thing out. In the story about Gareth, you will remember that the King would not start the Whitsun feast until an adventure was shown to him. That was simply the author's way of starting a new story – a new one at every Whitsun feast.

The first writer to turn Arthur the war-leader into Arthur the King was a monk, named Geoffrey, who was born at Monmouth in Wales. He wrote a book, more than eight hundred years after Arthur's death, which he called the *History of the British Kings*. Hardly any of it is true but it made the history of Britain so exciting that it became a bestseller – every copy handwritten – in 1138. He made Arthur a king who not only conquered France, Denmark and Norway, but became Emperor of Rome as well!

Geoffrey of Monmouth invented King Arthur, and the legend has been used by authors ever since. They have written dozens of books, poems, plays and films. It is a pity really that they are all about Arthur the King and the Knights of the Round Table. The gallant war-leader, galloping through the night at the head of his warriors, on the way to another battle against his country's enemies, is just as exciting. And a lot closer to the truth!

3 See Where it Happened

In the 'Inside Story' you saw that the real King Arthur was a British war-leader who became famous for his daring cavalry attacks against the invading Angles and Saxons. Arthur and his men lived a long, long time ago and after the hundreds of years that have passed since then there is very little evidence left about where and how they lived. Archaeologists have investigated several places to see if they can find objects associated with Arthur and you can read about what they have found in this chapter.

We do know, however, that many of the villas and roads left behind by the Romans were still standing during Arthur's lifetime, and although many were empty and derelict some at least were temporarily repaired and lived in by Britons. Excavations of these places have told us a great deal about the Roman way of life. Some of these sites are looked after by the National Trust.

When later writers made Arthur into a hero who had all kinds of make-believe adventures, his name became such a legend that people started to look for the places where these adventures took place. They tried to find the lake where the sword 'Excalibur' was thrown to the Lady of the Lake and the cave where he sleeps with his men until the day England should need them again. None of these things happened of course, but if you have a good imagination you will enjoy visiting some of the places associated with the legendary Arthur which are included in this chapter. You will find plenty to wonder at by imagining yourself back in the never-never land of Camelot with Lancelot, Gareth, and Shortlegs – even if the real King Arthur was a very different person!

Here now is a selection of all these places. Many are owned by the National Trust and they are marked like this *.

ENGLAND
AVON
Cadbury Camp, nr Clevedon
Cadbury has always been thought of as the most likely site of
Arthur's Camelot. It has recently been investigated by
archaeologists and you read about what they discovered in the
'Inside Story'. It was certainly never like the fairy-tale
Camelot of legend with a great stone castle.
Little Solsbury Hill*
Just outside Bath, between Batheaston and Swainswick, lies
Little Solsbury Hill. It is an ancient hill-fort which was once
occupied by Britons. As you saw in the 'Inside Story' some
people believe it might be the site of the famous Battle of
Badon. The evidence from excavations shows that it was
occupied between 300 BC and 100 BC, several hundred years
before Arthur.

CHESHIRE
Alderley Edge*
There is a legend about the wizard Merlin here. One day a
farmer was passing through the woods along Alderley Edge on
his way to Macclesfield market where he hoped to sell his fine,
white horse. In the woods he was stopped by Merlin. The
wizard offered to buy the horse but the farmer refused and
continued on his journey. When he arrived at Macclesfield
market nobody wanted to buy his horse so he had to return
with it through the wood. He met Merlin again and this time
the wizard led the farmer through the trees to a great rock.
As he touched it a pair of massive gates opened with a noise like
thunder which terrified the poor farmer. Merlin explained that
King Arthur and his knights lay sleeping in the cave beyond,
waiting until England was in danger and needed them again.
As they wanted one more white horse Merlin offered the
farmer a purse of gold for his. The poor man was so frightened
that he grabbed the purse and ran as fast as he could. The great
gates closed and the cave has never been seen since.

Today there is a wishing-well in the wood with this
inscription on it:

Drink of this and take thy fill,
For the water falls by the wizard's will.

CORNWALL
Dozmary Pool, Bodmin Moor
On Bodmin Moor near Jamaica Inn is a dark silent lake known as Dozmary Pool. There is a legend that this is the place where Arthur told Sir Bedevere to throw the great sword 'Excalibur' into the water. When he did so the Lady of the Lake caught the sword in her outstretched hand and took it down into the lake.

Loe Pool*
One mile east of Porthleven lies a freshwater lake called Loe Pool. It is separated from the sea by a narrow shingle beach. This is another place which claims to be where Sir Bedevere threw 'Excalibur' into the water.

Loe Pool

Tintagel

Slaughter Bridge, Camelford

By Camelford is Slaughter Bridge over the River Camel. Legend says that Arthur fought the great Battle of Camlann here against his nephew Mordred. The fighting was so fierce that the river flowed red with blood, Mordred was killed and Arthur mortally wounded. At the side of the river there is a stone slab which is supposed to mark Arthur's tomb. However, most versions of the legend say that Arthur was taken across the water to the Isle of Avalon where he was buried. The stone probably commemorates the site of a battle against the Saxons which was fought three hundred years later.

Tintagel*

Traditionally Tintagel is the place where Arthur was born. He is supposed to have spent his childhood in the castle which belonged to his father, King Uther Pendragon. Below the castle rock is Merlin's Cave. Another legend says that the infant Arthur was found by Merlin on the seashore below the castle. In fact Arthur lived a long time before the castle was ever built although the site was probably occupied by British monks while he was alive. The castle is owned by the Department of the Environment and the National Trust owns several areas of land around it as well as the Old Post Office in Tintagel village.

Trencrom Hill, nr Penzance*

The ancient British hill-fort on the top of Trencrom Hill has no story connecting it with King Arthur. Nevertheless it is a very good example of the kind of fort that the real Arthur and his men would have re-fortified in their campaign against the Angles and Saxons. Excavations have shown that it was certainly used about the time Arthur was alive.

Zennor Head*

The lovely views are not the only things you should look out for at Zennor Head. There is a flat stone here which is supposed to be where King Arthur dined with four other Cornish kings before a great battle against the English.

DORSET

Badbury Rings, nr Wimborne Minster

This is another place that has been proposed as the site of the Battle of Badon. It is a very impressive hill-fort with three circles of ramparts and ditches. There is a Roman road which connects it to the fort at Old Sarum near Salisbury and excavations have shown that it was occupied during Arthur's lifetime. It is certainly the sort of 'castle' Arthur, the British cavalry leader, would have recognised.

GLOUCESTERSHIRE

Chedworth Villa*

The years when Arthur was alive are usually called the Dark Ages. This is because it was a time when the great Roman civilisation had collapsed and people returned to living in a much more primitive way. You can understand this better at Chedworth Villa. About a hundred years before Arthur was born it was a great country villa with under-floor heating and hot baths where the rich Roman owners could relax. If you compare this with the illustration of the kind of house Arthur probably lived in on page 33 you will see how the times must have changed. When Arthur was alive the great villa at Chedworth was probably empty and derelict with weeds growing through its mosaic floors.

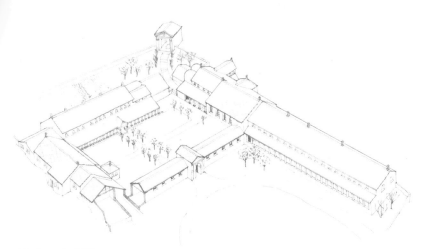

Chedworth Villa

HAMPSHIRE
Winchester Castle
In the Great Hall at Winchester Castle a 'Round Table' has hung for as long as anyone can remember. The names of Arthur and his knights are painted around the edge. Recently scientists investigated it to find out just how old it was. They decided it was probably made about 1340 and that it was built for King Edward III who was fascinated by the legend of Arthur. The 'Round Table' is almost the first thing we think of when we read about King Arthur. It is a fine idea to imagine Arthur at his Round Table with all his brave knights around him ready for the call to arms. Unfortunately it is a picture that was made up by later writers. The real King Arthur probably sat at a long rectangular table in a rough wooden hall full of smoke and animals!

HEREFORD AND WORCESTER
Dorstone, nr Hay-on-Wye
On Merbach Hill lies 'Arthur's Stone'. There are three legends about it so you can choose the one you like best. One says it marks the grave of a king who was killed when he started a fight with Arthur. Another that Arthur himself is buried here. The third says that Arthur fought and killed a giant here

and that the stone marks the giant's grave. The marks on the stones beside the grave are said to have been made by Arthur's knees as he knelt to pray after the fight.

NORTHUMBERLAND
Housesteads Fort, Hadrian's Wall*
Hadrian's Wall was built by the Romans as the northern limit of their occupation in Britain. When you visit it you can understand how strong they were as a military force. You can also understand how defenceless the British must have felt when they left. Housesteads Fort and the museum are owned by the National Trust but the Department of the Environment looks after them. There is a legend that Arthur lies sleeping in a cave beneath the wall awaiting the call to arms.

NORTH YORKSHIRE
Richmond Castle
There is a story here about a local potter whose name was Thompson. One day he was exploring near the castle when he found a secret tunnel that ran beneath it. At the far end he entered a huge cavern where King Arthur and his men lay sleeping. On a table near the entrance lay a sword and a horn. The potter picked up the horn and was about to blow it when the knights started to wake up. He was so frightened that he dropped the horn and ran away down the tunnel, as fast as he could. As he ran he heard a voice calling from the cavern:
Potter Thompson, potter Thompson,
If thou hadst drawn the sword or blown the horn,
Thou hadst been the luckiest man e'er born!

OXFORDSHIRE
Badbury Hill, nr Faringdon*
This is another Iron-Age hill-fort that has been suggested as the site of the Battle of Badon. When you stand inside the fort it is easy to imagine how the English must have felt with Arthur's cavalry camped below. It is impossible to know whether the Battle of Badon was really fought here, but we can at least be sure that it was on a hill very like Badbury.

Glastonbury Tor

SOMERSET

Glastonbury Tor*

If you look at Glastonbury Tor from a distance you will see that it stands out as a solitary hill like an island in the surrounding Somerset plain. In fact it was once in the middle of marsh and swamp-land which made it into a real island when flooded. This is why it has been identified as the 'Isle of Avalon' where Arthur was taken to be buried after the Battle of Camlann. There are certainly many associations with Arthur here. The tower on the top of the hill is all that remains of a church built hundreds of years after Arthur's lifetime, but there is evidence that there were people living here in the Dark Ages. At the bottom of the hill is 'The Chalice Well'. There is a legend that the Holy Grail (the cup that Jesus used at the Last Supper) was hidden here by Joseph of Arimathea. Many of the imaginary adventures of the Knights of the Round Table are about the search for the Holy Grail.

Nearby are the remains of Glastonbury Abbey (not owned by the National Trust). In the ruins there is a plaque which marks the supposed site of the grave of Arthur and Guinevere, his queen. It is possible that the monks in the monastery invented the story of Arthur's grave as a tourist attraction, but recent excavations have shown that it could well be the true site.

WEST SUSSEX
Cissbury Ring*
This is an ancient British hill-fort that was abandoned while the Romans were in the country. Later it was used again by the Britons, probably against the attacks of the English. Who knows, Arthur himself might have been among them.

WILTSHIRE
Liddington Castle, nr Swindon
This is yet another possible site for the Battle of Badon. Nearby is the village of Badbury and the Uffington White Horse.

WALES
DYFED
Bosherton, nr Pembroke
This lovely lily-covered lake is traditionally the place where Sir Bedevere threw 'Excalibur' into the water while Arthur lay dying at its edge. We have seen that there are several other places with the same claim – as it is only a fairy-story perhaps it is best to choose the prettiest!
Carmarthen
In the town there is an ancient tree known as 'Merlin's Oak'. It is traditionally the place where the wizard was born and he prophesied that when the tree fell Carmarthen would fall with it. You will see from the iron supports that the people of the town are taking no chances!

WEST GLAMORGAN
Craig y Ddinas Cave, nr Glyn Neath
There is a legend that Arthur and his men lie asleep in this cave. A Welsh shepherd was walking nearby carrying a stick made from hazelwood. He met a wizard who told him that if he

could lead the way to the tree he had cut it from he would find a great treasure. The shepherd agreed and when they reached the tree they found a secret passage leading to a cave. There was a bell at the entrance and inside they could see Arthur and his men sleeping beside a huge pile of treasure. The wizard told the shepherd that he could take as much as he could carry but that he must never touch the bell. If he did the warriors would wake up and demand 'Is it day?'. If that happened he should reply, 'No, sleep on' and all would be well. He was so greedy that he touched the bell twice as he collected the treasure but both times he remembered the correct answer. The third time he touched it he was so busy with his work that he forgot all about the reply. The knights rose up and beat him so badly that he never dared return, even for all that treasure!

SCOTLAND
CENTRAL LOTHIAN
Camelon, nr Falkirk
There is a monument on the bank of the River Carron near Camelon which is known as Arthur's Oven. The battle of Camlann is sometimes said to have been at the Roman town of Camelon. Although there is no evidence that Arthur ever came as far as Scotland.
Edinburgh
No visitor to Edinburgh can miss the great rock outcrop known as 'Arthur's Seat'. Many of the legends about Arthur speak of him as a giant and this is certainly a seat for a very large person indeed! In fact it is all that is left of an ancient volcano.

BORDERS
Eildon Hills, nr Melrose
Beneath these brooding hills is yet another cave where Arthur is supposed to lie sleeping with his men.

MAP OF PLACES
MENTIONED IN CHAPTER 3

National Trust sites

Other places of interest

Camelon

Edinburgh

Eildon Hills

Housteads
Fort

Richmond
Castle

Alderley
Edge

Dorstone

Carmarthen

Craig y Ddinas

Chedworth
Villa

Badbury Hill

Bosherton

Little
Solsbury
Hill

Liddington Castle

Glastonbury
Tor

Winchester
Castle

Cissbury
Ring

Cadbury Castle

Badbury
Rings

Tintagel

Slaughter Bridge,
Camelford

Zennor
Head

Dozmary
Pool

Trencrom
Hill

Loe Pool